Poems to Share

Poems by Leroy F. Jackson
Selected by Kathleen Paton
Illustrated by Cornelius Van Wright

Checkerboard Press 🏶 New York

Copyright © 1990, 1937 Checkerboard Press.
Selected poems by Leroy F. Jackson originally published by Rand McNally & Company
under the title *The Jolly Jingle Picture Book*. All rights reserved.
ISBN: 002-689516-1 Printed in the United States of America.
0 9 8 7 6 5 4 3 2 1

CANTALOUPE FOR BREAKFAST

Cantaloupe for breakfast,
Honey and a bun!
Get your shoes and
   stockings on
And run, run, run!

You're slow as half a
   dozen snails,
The folks have all begun!
There's cantaloupe for
   breakfast,
Honey and a bun!

POKY PARSONS

Who was late to school
   today?
Poky, Poky Parsons.
Who was tardy
   yesterday?
Poky, Poky Parsons.
Never known to be on
   time,
Wouldn't hurry for a
   dime,
Poky, Poky Parsons.

NEW SHOES

Mother bought Polly a new pair of shoes
With a shiny part over the toes,
And now she must keep them close by her
    at night
And wear them wherever she goes.

A REAL SHOW

If you want to see a real
    show,
Hurry — now's your
    chance!
Mary's going to sing a song
And Ruth is going to dance.

And maybe Bob will play a
    tune
And Stanley whistle some,
Tell you what, you're
    missing it;
You really ought to come.

WON'T YOU BUY A PRETTY FLOWER?

Won't you buy
    a pretty flower?
Won't you buy a rose?
The fairies keep
    their treasure
In the garden where
    it grows,
Its leaves were born
    in loveliness,
A virtue with it goes.
Won't you buy
    a pretty flower?
Won't you buy a rose?

A CHICKEN-SPILL

As I was running down the
    hill
I took a dreadful chicken-
    spill;
I knocked my knees and
    skinned my pate
And landed right at
    Grandma's gate.

THE WONDER LADY

The Wonder Lady came to
the beach
Before the sun was up
And carried off the ocean
In a little china cup.

FUN

I love to hear a lobster laugh,
Or see a turtle wiggle,
Or poke a hippopotamus
And see the monster giggle,
Or even stand around at
night
And watch the mountains
wriggle.

WHAT?

What is moister than an
oyster?
What is slicker than an eel?
What is flatter than a
platter?
What is rounder than a
wheel?

DOWN AT HENRY HUNTER'S PLACE

Down at Henry Hunter's
place
The caterpillars sing,
And all the cats and
collie dogs
Have feathers in the
spring.

And every night the lions
climb
Upon the house and
roar,
And the grizzly bears
come round and
peddle
Peanuts at the door.

And panthers come and
drink the milk.
It's kind of funny,
though
I'm sure it must be true
all right
'Cause Henry told me so.

MISS TOPSY TURVY

Miss Topsy Turvy lives alone
On Dizzy Dazzle Street.
She wears her slippers on her
    hands
And mittens on her feet.
She takes a broom and
    dustpan
To the garden when she hoes.
She sits and smells a bowl of
    soup
And gobbles down a rose.
She sleeps upon a towel at
    night
And washes with a sheet,
Miss Topsy Turvy, Crazy Cat,
On Dizzy Dazzle Street.

RAINBOW, RAINBOW

Rainbow, rainbow, coming
    down
Right in the very edge of
    town,
Here's my hat and coat to
    hold
While I run and get the
    pot of gold.

AN UMBRELLA WENT WALKING

An umbrella went walking with
    Old Missus Stout
Because it was raining that day;
But all of a sudden the sunshine
    came out
And chased the umbrella away.

BABY BESS

I think that Baby Bess
    believes
That kittens live on lettuce
    leaves;
That grapes and oranges
    galore
Should grow behind the
    kitchen door;
And peanuts, sausages,
    and cheese
May all be picked from
    apple trees;
That dishes quarrel,
    pumpkins fight,
And houses walk about at
    night.
All the tales that Tilly
    weaves
Little Baby Bess believes.

I'D LIKE TO BE A SPOTTED COW

If I weren't what I am just
   now
I'd like to be a spotted cow,
With long green grass to
   crop and chew
And nothing else on earth to
   do.

And if I couldn't manage
   that
I think I'd be a tommy cat;
I'd have a host of rats to
   fight
And two big starey eyes at
   night.

And if I had to pass that by,
I guess I'd rather be a fly
And live on fudge and
   candy hearts
And juice that leaks from
   apple tarts.

Sometimes I think I'd
rather be
A monkey in a melon tree,
Eating pickles by the pail
Or slowly swinging by my
tail.

Or I might go down south
somewhere
And be a lion in his lair;
I'd roam around the jungle
floor,
Then stand up on a rock
and roar.

But eeny, meeny, Peter,
Paul;
I guess that maybe after all
If I weren't what I am just
now
I'd rather be a spotted cow.

ISN'T IT GRAND?

Isn't it grand
To sit in the sand
And dig for pirate's gold,
And maybe bring up
A mermaid's cup
And give it to baby to hold?

Isn't it grand
To walk on the sand
And make little holes with your toes,
Or watch the big ship
Start off on a trip
To Spain or wherever it goes?

HOW A PUPPY GROWS

I think it's very funny
The way a puppy grows
A little on his wiggle-tail,
A little on his nose,
A little on his tummy
And a little on his ears;
I guess he'll be a dog all right
In half a dozen years.

I LIKE THE MOON

I like the moon;
    he always gives
A quiet kind of light;
I wonder if the sleepyhead
Can stay awake all night.

FLUFFY, RUFFY, ROSY

Fluffy, ruffy, rosy,
Tucked up nice and cozy,
Plenty cover for her bed,
Pretty pillow for her head,
Washed and waiting to be fed—
Fluffy, ruffy, rosy.

GRANNY FADDLE

Granny Faddle, Granny Faddle,
My, oh, my!
I never knew there was
Such huckleberry pie;
Granny Faddle, Granny Faddle,
Don't you peek,
I'm going to kiss you
On your dear old cheek.

GOING HOME

Now we're far away from
   Grandma's
  On the train:
Out among the woods and
   rivers
  And the grain.

If the train doesn't stop for
   dinner
Or to put some water in her,
We'll be home before the
   sky
  Begins to rain.

BILLY AND TILLY

Billy sat on the floor
And Tilly sat on a chair,
But 'twas hardly a minute before
They were into each other's hair,
For Tilly wanted to sit on the floor
And Billy to sit on a chair.

SUGAR

I want sugar on my oatmeal
And sugar on my bread,
I'll turn into a sugar stick
Some day, my grandma
    said.
Sugar by the spoonful
And sugar by the bowl—
I wouldn't trade a lump of
    sugar
For a buttered roll.

ISN'T IT STRANGE?

Shoes have tongues,
But cannot talk;
Tables have legs,
But cannot walk,
Needles have eyes,
But cannot see;
Chairs have arms,
But they can't hug me!